BEYOND THE STONE

BEYOND THE STONE
Poems of Tribute & Remembrance

JAMES EVERETT KIBLER, JR.

Beyond The Stone: Poems of Tribute & Remembrance
Copyright© 2025 by James Everett Kibler, Jr.

ALL RIGHTS RESERVED. No part of this publication may be reproduced, distributed, or transmitted in any form or by any means, including photocopying, recording, or other electronic or mechanical methods, or by any information storage and retrieval system without the prior written permission of the publisher, except in the case of very brief quotations embodied in critical reviews and certain other non-commercial uses permitted by copyright law.

Produced in the Republic of South Carolina by

Green Altar Books,
an imprint of Shotwell Publishing LLC

Post Office Box 2592

Columbia, South Carolina 29202

www.ShotwellPublishing.com

Cover: Barrow Wheary plays traditional tunes on a centuries old Virginia fiddle at the poet's home, 27 December 2023. Photo by Patty Russell.

ISBN: 978-1-963506-30-3

FIRST EDITION

10 9 8 7 6 5 4 3 2 1

"First Whippoorwill" and "City Billboards" first appeared in *Yearbook of the Poetry Society of South Carolina*. "Still Life" and "Davis College, Spring 1964" appeared in *Columbia Metropolitan Magazine*. "For Dove and Flag," "Monuments," "Deep Southern Summer," and "Meditation in an Evil Time" appeared in *Abbeville Institute Journal*. "A Seed Is Memory" first appeared in an early version in *Tiller* (2016). Several of *The Chauncey Poems* first appeared in *The Education of Chauncey Doolittle* (2003). "Rowan Oak, June 1998" and "To My Father Who Made the Choice to Stay" are from my collection *Poems from Scorched Earth* (2000). "Chauncey Longs for Home in Spring" is revised from *Poems from Scorched Earth* and *Pembroke Magazine* (2001). "In Faulkner's Garden" first appeared in *Faulkner the Southerner & the Continuity of Southern Letters* (2023). The remainder are newly published.

To The Reader

The collection's four sections were written roughly in the order presented here. The poems of Section I, "Openings," resulted from visits to England and Italy in the 1970s and early 80s when I was finding my place in Western culture. Venice, most particularly, got me to writing poetry in earnest, hence the section's title.

Section II, "Agrarian Poems," pays tribute to the figures of the Fugitive-Agrarian movement and reflects my move from city to country in 1989 and the period in which I wrote my Agrarian chronicle *Our Fathers' Fields*. It is interesting to note the irony that "Message on an Old Chalkboard," which honours Agrarian John Donald Wade, was rejected in spring 1982 by *The Georgia Review*, which he founded.

Section III, "The Chauncey Poems," was composed by my fictional alter-ego, poet Chauncey Doolittle, a central character of my novel series published from 2004 to 2016. They were set at my plantation home.

Section IV, "Airlift," was occasioned by helicopter airlift for heart surgery in 2021 and the aftermath of that experience. I may be the only poet who has watched his heart beat during surgery and lived to write about it.

The overarching theme of the collection is respectful remembrance—with subjects ranging from my literary fathers to flesh and blood kin, hearth, and home. A primary homage in sections 2, 3, and 4 is to the land itself.

Responses to specific events can be traced in all four sections. "Southern Son," inspired by Yeats's "Irish Airman," was written after the death of my father in 1996. "Sassetta" and "War Protest" were in response to the war in Iraq. "Contemplation" and "Monuments" were written in 2021 at the height of the frenzy to destroy monuments. Two poems followed visits to Faulkner's home in 1970 and 1988.

Modern concerns such as the corrosive effects of empire, urbanisation, globalisation, and the 20th Century's never-ending wars with their Amazons of blood are subjects appearing throughout.

Of writing poetry in advanced age, I quote the master Yeats:

> An aged man is but a paltry thing
> A tattered coat upon a stick, unless
> Soul clap its hands and sing, and louder sing
> For every tatter in its mortal dress.

No one has put it better.   January 2025

To the Memory of
ENNIS REES
Who coaxed the spark from the flint.

The South has memory,
showing itself through landscape and character,
and that is better for poetry than anything else
except that which is poetry itself—desire.
— Padraic Colum

Epigraph for *The Yearbook of the Poetry Society of South Carolina*, 1921

Proem
(Written Four Centuries after the Folio)

As said the murdered father's ghost, "Remember Me,"
As on St. Crispin's Crispin's Day
That we remembered are.
So Hamlet passes to his friend his dying words
To tell the tale,
All art exists in Memory
Memorials to the thing we are
Or ought to be.
The oldest bards all knew
The fabric always must be strong
To line a song
To tell us who we are
And that they did their duty
Passed it on
With duty now to sing the song.
It is but *pietas* after all
The door swings equally both way,
The duty to be courageous, brave
And then remembered in new day.

Contents

To The Reader, vii

Proem, xi

I. OPENINGS

Venice 1982, 1

Spanish Steps, 5

Meditation On Sassetta's *Magi* In A Time Of War, 6

Demodokos:, 10

Homage To Dante, 12

At The Haskell Plot, Trinity Cemetery, Abbeville, South Carolina In The Year 2000, 14

Blue Girl, 16

To My Father, Who Made The Choice To Stay, 17

A Southern Son Receives The Flag Of Empire At The Grave Of His Father, 20

Homage To Thomas MacDonagh, 21

President Davis In Chains, 22

Let Dixie Remember, 24

I Am The South, 26

On Egdon. 1 November 1982, 27

In Faulkner's Garden, 10 May 1970, 28

For Simms, 30

Monuments (Beyond The Stone), 31

Rowan Oak, June 1998, 32

Contemplation In An Evil Time, 34

A Nation Once Again, 36

Beneath The Starry Cross:, 38

Revenant At Dawn, 40

For William Butler Yeats, 42

The Master of Hampton, 45

If Time, 46

II. Agrarian Poems

The Happy Isle, 49

Hoc Erat In Votis, 50

The "Hercules and Antæus" of Pollaiuolo, 51

Message On An Old Chalkboard, 52

In Memoriam Andrew Lytle (1902-1995), 54

City Skylines, 55

Nine-Eleven 2001, 56

For Dove and Flag, Grandpa Connelly's Mules, 58

The Butchering, 60

Miss Ophelia's Garden, 62

Drought, 64

The Broken, 65

An Elegy For All Ruined Gardens, 66

On He Who Plants The Winter Tree, 67

Tree Poem In Winter, 68

A Tribute To Jim Clark, 69

Elegy For Tanya Berry's Hillside, 70

Sonnet For Wendell Berry, 72

Sonnet. Beyond Wordsworth, 73

Davis College, Spring 1964, 74

A Walk With Michaux At Ballylee, 76

First Whippoorwill, 79

Still Life.Pavia With Hummingbird. , 80

Geologists Say, 82

Bounty, 83

Old Farmer Lyman's Maxims For The Modern Time, 84

A Seed Is Memory, 87

Written In The Centre Of A National Forest, 88

City Billboards, 89

An Elegy For The Whitmire Pig, 90

Sprawl-Mart: A Mock Heroic, 92

The Hidden Wound, 94

Swallowtail Summer, 95

Needs, 96

Following The Santa Float, 97

Dream Poem In An Old House, 98

Golden Girl, 99

The Teacher Observes His Students During An Exam, 100

Puritan, 101

Doggeril I. Musings On A Pseudo-Southern Bard, 102

Doggeril II. The Same Subject (In A Moment Of Pique), 103

Homage To Ezra Pound. War Protest, Athens, Georgia, February 2003, 104

Cage Country, 106

War Protest II, March 2003, 107

III. CHAUNCEY'S POEMS OLD AND NEW

Druid Poem, 111

Chauncey Reflects On His Verse, 112

Chauncey Pays Tribute To His Laurel Tree, 113

Chauncey Envisions A Fire-Tree, 114

Rhymes For The Old Men Who Plant Trees, 115

Old House, 116

Summer Morning Dawns On The Plantation, 117

Chauncey Longs For Home In Spring, 118

Chauncey's Spring Song For An Old House, 119

Chauncey Remembers, 120

Mutability, 121

Winter Solstice, 122

Lost In The Thorny Wood, 123

Full Christmas Moon, 124

Chauncey's Song, 126

Chauncey Sees His First Cranesbill In His Winter Woods, 128

Rain In March, 129

Persimmon Fall, 130

In The Short Rows. Chauncey's Poem On His Fortieth Birthday, 131

Chauncey In Praise of Writer's Block, 132

Chauncey Observes His Pumpkin Vines In June, 134

The Times. Chauncey Vents To A Friend, 136

Chauncey To His Books, 137

Chauncey To His Stray, 138

The Countryman's Song At Summer Dawn, 139

The Ploughman's Reverie, 140

Gardenias In Bloom, 141

Chauncey Casts His Pearls. A Variation Of Matthew 7, 142

Chauncey's Rendering From The Seventh Century Gælic, 143

Chauncey's Inscription For His Wood, 144

IV. Airlift

In Praise of The Romantics, 147

This Hand , 148

Airlift, 149

What Wonder Of A Year, 150

The Patient Watches His Heart On Ultrasound, 151

Long View, 152

Paradox, 153

Carpet's Figure, 154

Lines In Winter. , 155

Written In The Year 2021, 156

December Song, 157

September Song. In Praise Of The Well-Worn Path, 158

Plough Monday., 160

Hallowed, 162

Fair Southern Land, 164

Dixie Battle Hymn, 166

Deep Southern Summer Written At Midnight, 169

The Land Remains, 170

And The Poem Goes On, 172

Southern Poets Sing Your Songs, 173

Good Friday, 174

Easter Prayer, 175

Land of Song, 176

Spring Canticle, 178

First Poem, 179

About the Author, 181

I.

OPENINGS

Venice
1982

I.
From A Fourth Story Room

In dark of just awaking,
Dim shuttered light of moon
Brings haze of waters flowing
Round cabinets,
And beds ,
All shadowed objects,
Prying into corners of the room.
These the land spaces,
A maze of the just barely firm,
Of the melting stone,
And the walls all awash
With the movement
Of frail craft remembered of noon.

For all the night long
The voice of the waters lapping
At less solid base,
Has made insubstantial
The fading brief pageant
In purple and gold.

With half-day, the oil and the fume
Of mechanical bustle to markets
Will come and will render more potent
The action of tide,
And take through the haze-tender gold of the day
The lapping incessant of waters
To seek out all corners
And never relent
'Til day is well spent.

So at night,
Once again,
The motion of waters around me
Drifts all to dark moon-spangled sea,
Here in the world of the waters, by water born.
And we truly such stuff dreams are made on,
Find all made less solid
In solvent
Of ashes and brine.

Your collonades fading,
Your banners, stone lions
Dissolving,
Yet ever, like part of the sea
That all carry in blood,
I will carry you forth

In the motion of waters
Felt inland,
Forever awash
In the brine-bath of time.

II.
Isle Of The Dead

The day weds the soil to the waters,
Commits clay to waves.
The floating strange isle in the distance,
Its terra-cotta warmth
In sun-shimmer,
Glows against and out of the blue,
A soft mirage
Between sky and sea
To vanish soon.
The Rialto brings me
Flowing by—
Changing monuments
Shifting, dissolving, with passing,
Your cedars
The smoke of funeral pyres,
Dark twisting cloud columns
Uplifting,
Eternally pointing
To sky

III.
TORCELLO DUOMO

In Murano
The blower of glass
Makes bubbles of air.

On kind-weeded island
Settles and nests
In dove-colored bisque
Torcello Duomo
No less fragile fantastic
Than bubble of glass,
But deep-rooted,
Tenacious—
Enduring, true spirit of place.

❖

Spanish Steps
(For John Keats, Rome 1981)

I

From sacrifice of innocents
Do we all survive—
How softly sweet
To languish here,
Oh lamb,
Beside this open sweep of stone,
To see on summer day
Your Jacob's Ladder move from dappled reds
To brightest blue, with spirits musical.

II

To sell our wares of bead and bread,
Bathe brown-backed, baked, in August sun,
To breathe in clouds of pungent incense,—
Here gather all
To sound of lute and the cither
With sandals worn paper thin.—
Celebrants all.
We gather you in.

❖

Meditation On Sassetta's *Magi* In A Time Of War

I

Siena's light is there
Reflects on Persian sand;
Storks fly squadron in the steely blue,
Another pair stands gangly on a fortress hill;
Storks and stars work anciently at births.
The Magi follow star of course.
It shines like gilded splatter-blot, full Byzantine
But strangely placed off-centre like the times,
Decoration more than guide.
(The painting is a part;
Its triptych members disjunct far—
An ocean in between—
So fitting in a fractured day).
A falcon sits on arm imperial,
Pigeons unsuspecting fly.
Crusader castle fortress gate behind.
Kings' entourage is many more than three,
The size of unit winding off to war.
What stops the eye
Is proudest show of gift,
Not gold or frankincense or myrrh
But on its donkey back,
Splendid laid upon a carpet richly arabesque,
Like Cleopatra on her barge reclined,

A wizened monkey with a tail of wire—
So strange, exotic, stretched out there
As if in setting rare
A rarer jewel still,
Fit gift for newborn king indeed!
Spice routes would doubtless have allowed,
And Caspar, Melchior and Balthazar
All three would understand:
A king must be amused;
He has so much already that he needs.
A Sienese in flushest time would also understand.
So there the monkey sits
For all the world to see.

II

It works, though strange enough, this gift of theirs
But still one wonders if Sassetta
Had bad translation from the Greek
Reading monkey for the myrrh,
Or if some tired-eyed anchorite in freezing cell
Late copying by fading light
With numb cold hand
Had nodded in brown hood.
No matter what the case,
I take Sassetta at his word
The Magi made a gift of monkey to our Lord.

III

It gives us much to muse upon.
What would have Mary thought? And said?
And Joseph changing hourly swaddling clothes?
No doubt they had two sets of comments there at manger side
Most gracious, gentle always as her wont,
The Mother thanked the Magi in sincerest tone,
But she and Joseph when the three were gone
Must still have had a different take on things.
"What are we going to do with this monkey?"
Joseph must have asked perplexed
And Mary sadly may have said
"Diapers would have been a timely gift,
There's just so many swaddling clothes."
Then later, Joseph in a moment of sharp pique:
"I thought that angel had said myrrh;
I'll never trust a one of them again."
"Now, Joseph," Mary would have said to calm him down.
"Still," he replied,
"The shepherds seemed much wiser than the kings.
These lambs are what we need
And goat milk for our babe, and cheese.
That bag of meal, those warmest skins,
Will keep together souls and bodies through the cold."

Joseph eyed the monkey as he spoke.
The creature lolled on carpet that the kings had left behind
And reached to catch and eat a fly.
"I'll bet he'll soon get fleas," our Joseph said;
And still he grumbled past the lantern lighting time:
"Shepherds never would have even *thought* of this!"
And Joseph showed his wisdom good as Magi gold—
As out on lonely hills, the shepherds watched their sheep,
Gave quiet meditation to the stars
And made no wars
And stood a lasting pattern for our Lord.

❖

Demodokos:
For Ennis Rees, Who Introduced Me To Homer

Homer had it right
About the primacy of song—
The song that does remembering
Attaching then to now.
"The gods," he said,
"Did this, this iliad of war
And spun destruction of a place
For sake of singing men to come."
Their song the purpose thus divine
Fulfilling gods' decree.
Destruction came so that a song could be.

Demodokos,
The loyal singer dressed in hides
Could bring the guest to tears
Rememb'ring well his warrior deeds
So powerfully described.
The silver-studded chair his seat
Against the marble shaft
That held the palace up,
Where hung his clear-toned lyre
On peg above his head,
His song the stranger's very deeds.

With his big hands
Odysseus took his purple cloak
And pulled it cross his face
So that Phæacians could not see his tears
Recalling all the agony as fresh as were the year.
So *this* is what the suffering was for.
To be remembered in a song that lives.
Alcinous *only* saw the tear
And he from this Odysseus knew.

❖

Homage To Dante

Concerning His Statue in Florence

The eighteen feet of marble
Will not do
To bring the banished home
Or balance sentence to an exile's death.
Too heavy on the scales
To rob of line and conduit to the skies
Chimneyed from prismatic roof of Baptistry
With fires of Easter tide
Uniting all in civic bond
To never see.
"My beautiful St. John," said he.
It was a banishment severe,
The longing heart in alien wood
To pine among the foreign pines.

To gnaw upon a severed head
Throughout eternity
Severe damnation not enough.
To sever soul from home
Reserves the spot Inferno's own.
It takes a more than Beatrice
To banish all Firenze's enmity.

A marble statue will not do
Nor marvel of Duomo's lantern raised.
The debt remains unpaid,
Remains the curse on Arno's tide,
No penitential effigy relieves.

At The Haskell Plot, Trinity Cemetery, Abbeville, South Carolina In The Year 2000

Pro patria mori—

Old Horace had it right,
As right as Wilfred Owen wrong.
The crucial hinge
On which the matter swings
Is *Patria*—
No large inflated abstract of a land,
No patented ideal,
But father's verdant fields
Where beech trees with the broken tops
Run down to Mincio—
Where Horace and Virgilius
Meet by its waters still undammed
And clap each other's shoulders
With poet's hands.

How sadly fallen since an empire's time.
No wonder that an Owen
Disillusioned falls
His will to fail.

Beyond The Stone

Standing 'mongst her fallen slain
Dulce et Decorum est, Pro Patria Mori
The stone carved ribbon claims.
The Haskell brothers
Killed short days apart,
The bones of one to stand for two,
The distant bones in sands away.
Still linked they are
With granite twin-crossed swords,
Linked double laurel wreaths.

Great trees drop leaves
As if in spattered tribute
To the blood they shed.

They knew their *Patria*,
Their family and fields—
No doubting of the right
To stand between invader
And a mother's hearth.

Our tribute seeds a lyric bounty full
In tragic contrast to diminished time,
Engendering no faith,
Deserving of no rhyme.

❖,

Blue Girl

For My Father Who Remembered the War

Amid débris of broken lives in flood
She stands in winter eddying of war
Fixed point in blue
As seen from troop-trains hurtling home—
Bare arms now purpling cold.
My father to warm her in memory—
Lone delicate figure
Ice-etched in late Alpine snow.
Unheeded, unheeding,
Sleep-walking her dream of the cold,

She moved to the last in old soldier's mem'ry,
And now in his son's,
Through decades encircling
Returning; etched emblem of era of ice
Numbed century of blood-draining strife:
Palest frail figure in blue.

To My Father, Who Made The Choice To Stay

A wandering people is more or less a barbarous one.
– William Gilmore Simms

One great and burning question
Dogged us from the start—
That is, since first turned from the flaming gates,
The question, great divide,
Much bigger than the Rockies of a continent,
Is whether go or stay,
Of whether sink down roots or snap them off.
To go relieves us from responsibility.
Community requires some giving in and giving up,
Some paying back, some gentle ties
That often inconvenience love of self alone.
To stay takes bigger act of faith
Than venturing unknown.

The known is venture far and wide and deep enough,
Propels us from our self of sense alone
Which is diminished smallest world of all.
Our going selves will move in vacuum of the sense,
A bubble of the pleasures charting restless cross the land
And never touching earth but to consume and blight.

It is the image of our day of our dis-ease
Hermetically to seal off death and tears,
To move our lives about on wheels, with gears,
A Greyhound, AMTRAC, TWA,
We hover over land but never stay.
Abstraction never finds a proper home.
Emotion is the kind that comes from screen
That flickers in uneasy dots of light and dark.
Death is the thing most feared—embarrassment,
Reminding us of disobedience at the first.
Death ties us down and makes us deal with earth—
No longer virtual reality—
No pleasures are encouraged in the grave,
So we will stay at last you may be sure
No matter what the choice in life.

But staying all along we daily deal with death
As part of a procession and a whole,
The only wheel that matters
Where we enter immortality
That links us hand and hand through time
With past that's deeper than our own bloodline.

We enter genius of the place
With every day that's parceled out;
Our feet are on a soil that's rich with memory.

Our footsteps there erased, we linger on another plane
That's registered in a nuance of a voice
Or smile or moisture of an eye,
The sound of wind in trees
Or water over rocks
Of phoebe calling from her mossy nest at door
Or rafters of the porch.
From wholeness anchored in the place,
From joy of living in community,
We take a health and ease
And gladly, sharply sing our stay
Like wrens above the door
Incarnation sure and pure.

❖

A Southern Son Receives The Flag
Of Empire At The Grave Of His Father

He was a World War vet,
And not a willing one
But torn from out a peaceful Southern home
To cross the seas
Where risk of death would benefit his people none.
By grace of God returned,
He was forgotten straight
And so his people too.

The years have crept
To this dark gash in Southern clay—
One gash upon so many more
These hundred forty years.
The son stands on its beetling edge,
A people brought to precipice,
The folded spangled shroud of kith and kin
Clamped burning in its plastic, gripper-snapped,
Beneath the sweating arm.

❖

Homage To Thomas MacDonagh

"I have seldom known a man in whom the instinct of friendship was so true, nor one who was so prepared to use himself in the service of a friend. I do not think he had any other ambition than to write good verse and to love his friends, and the pleasure he found in these two acts was the sole profit I ever knew him to seek or to get." An officer who witnessed his and his friends' executions said,"They all died well, but MacDonagh died like a Prince."

—James Stephens

Now with the autumn roses fades another year
    And one less left to live.
  And all our roses must forever die,
In all the world there lives no lasting thing,
  No thing in all the world; and you and I
    Mere ghostly summers long since dead,
Turn to our winters with no second spring.
Then all that's left is faint remembering.
The only stays, that you remembered are—
    Your words to say you were.

President Davis In Chains

The lamp was always lit
So I could sleep but fitfully
They'd let me have no chair
And only narrow cot,
No screen for chamber pot.
My worn and skimpy coat
Was all they would alot.

In silence I could bear
The torture of the lamp, the cold,
The oozing damp and mold,
But when they ushered in the four
I knew the game.
One held the manacle and chain.
Three pinioned me to floor.

They did not get it easy.
Spent and fevered ill,
I kicked three of them senseless
Til
They ushered in four more.
So me they put in chains.

I hid my chained-down limbs
Beneath my one rough sheet.
Ashamed, subdued they thought.
Instead, I saw in secret sight
All people in their land
Were wearing chains much worse than mine
Their children and their children too o'er time.
I looked—
the grinning guards had stronger chains than mine.
It made the cutting steel
A glory and a crown.

Let Dixie Remember
Sung to the tune of "Let Erin Remember" by Thomas Moore

Let Dixie remember the days of old
'Ere her faithless sons betrayed her,
When proudly flew her flag from domes,
She resisted the lies of invaders,
When her history proud not belied or profaned
With her truth undimmed by anger
'Ere the rarest gem of the Western world
Was set in the crown of the stranger.

Let Dixie remember the days of old
'Fore the days of bold heroes were over,
When her sons were too proud to be bought and sold,
Wore the grey not the green of the soldier.
When her honour never went for the price of gold
And all comfort and ignorance sold her
When she knew her strengths and rights of old
And she brooked not the sins of her sellers.

Let Dixie remember the days of old
With her knowledge of right to guard her,
With her sons and daughters assured of the truth
That her freedom is promised forever.
Let her gallantry be reborn as bold star
To lighten the dark of disaster
To give then a birthright of freedom for all
And preserve then the cross on the altar.

18 January 2004

I Am The South

(After Padraig Pearse, Misé Eire)

I am the South:
I am older than Helena's dead.

Great my glory:
I that bore Jackson and Lee.

Great now my shame:
My children that bartered a mother.

Great now my sorrow:
My true sons betrayed.

I am the South:
I am lonelier than Helena's dead.

On Egdon.
1 November 1982

*"...there remained only the imperturbable
countenance of the heath."*
—*Thomas Hardy*

Dark face,
Wide waste,
Your tragic truths endure.
Mad Tom's withdrawn
And Lear's quavered out
His last heart-cracked line,
Fragile Eustacia,
Outspinning,
Has restlessly passed
In swirl of a pool,
Dark blossom to flower in death;
Mother's hurt,
So felt by son,
Shattered quite
To shadow of page,
Pain lost in numbness of time.
Man passing ephemeral
From face that's eternal:
Pale moths to flit
In moonlight fern
And then in midnight flame
To burn.

❖

In Faulkner's Garden, 10 May 1970

It made triangle:
Pear tree leaning hard toward death;
The base, home's soil itself,
Hypoteneuse a polished cedar prop
Placed at a cleft to shore tree up.

The man who placed support
Often spoke of props
Helping man endure, prevail.
It was his cast of mind,
This shoring up of things
Bespeaking struggle in a struggling time.
He knew the process well.
The fall-out ashes of war-wasted town
No doubt had fed the tree
That may have felt the glare of August 1864.
It was a link in time,
This living-tissued monument,
Become the artifice eternity
In shaping, shoring hands,
A more than prop—a solid pyramid immutable.

Half century has passed.
Today the tree is gone
Succumbed to drought, or wind,
Or just a gardener's tidying up.
But it endures like truth
Because I saw it there,
Still see it clear in memory—
The one green joyous shoot atop,
Singing life in leaves though leaves were few;
And in these lines
Prop it again
With cedar-penciled memory,
Poor words the leaves of life
Replenishing the branch
Into a hemispheric tree
Bearing perfect fruit.

For Simms

In Tribute to Yeats

Gold-beaten bird
From jewelled bough
Trilling past, the passing, and to come,
Bees among the woodland vines
Whippoorwill's sharp clarion call
At dusk and dawn,
Bob-white in golden fields of fall,
Mockingbird's song.
Bunting an animate rainbow on wings,
Hound voices off far on Edisto,
Waves on Ashley's green shore
Woodlands sighing in summer's deep storm.

Taking their music up
To figure in gold
Past jeweller's skill,
Singing on to all time.
Lords and Ladies to come
Listening rapt
In Lapis green glow
Of golden Byzantium.

❖

Monuments
(Beyond The Stone)

Their carven words all testify
Of then and now to future time
That these were they who kept the cause
Was given them by fathers past
And living still in coursing blood.

They token men
True to their lineage.
To sons they left high honour and the land,
A legacy of action speaking still.

Let stone forever warn
The men who sit in marble halls
That sires are only seeming dead.
They hover near in grey embattled line
Beneath torn pennons' scarlet flash;
And principles remain
Beyond our flesh and time,
Beyond the stone.

Rowan Oak, June 1998

High-circling hawk was clue:
This is your home
My kinsman true.
Allspice bush in cedared yard
Gave evidences too
Green world and blue,
The red-tail, far too far to hear
Its brittle cry
(But at my home outside the window high,
Persimmon perched, we're eye to eye—
Same hawk, same cry.)

I leave the hawk behind
And walk the porch to door unscreened.
The whitewashed walls glow with their inner light,
The khaki, tan, and white,
The well-washed cotton green,
The woods a screen
Of all we've left behind.
It is your footprint that I trace—
House and hawk and light and door unscreened
The trabiated transom same
As at my own fond home.

I search you here and find,
The portal arch of turnings,
And returnings,
Living with the dead and yet unborn,
To mirror still this day of origin,
The now of all-time, past and yet to come.
All time is one.

Contemplation In An Evil Time
Written in the Year 2021

Hampton, our stalwart Wade,
As wily as Odysseus in war
As full of rage for truth in time of fraud
As any celebrated Greek,
He saw his son fall at his feet,
Kissed him a hard farewell
In manner Hector or Odysseus
Would bring to tears,
Turned back to battlefield
Which he controlled
With more of righteous anger
Than Achilles ever knew.
Remains the story of the power in his arm
That wielded on his mount
A burnished broadsword Roman style.

He fought until the end
To time when Appomattox
Was already distanced past
To build again
A burned and tragic home,
A hero to his land
Who sent him to defend again
In nation's torn and still divided halls
Until unseated by a demagogue.

His friends assured,
"Your State will send you back
Through legislative act,
If you but say the word."
But he said "No. The seat to be *bestowed*
Not sought and not begged for."
The heavy Roman sword
But takes a muscled arm to even lift,
That split a skull in twain to shoulder blade
Is still with us today
If but display.
The marvel is its heaviness to hand—
Far heavier than the head that wears a crown
In time that bears a weakling, pandering brood
With no such giants in the land.

James Everett Kibler, Jr.

A Nation Once Again
Sung to the melody of the Irish ballad "The Croppy Boy"

One April morning as I heard
The gathering music from the birds,
The birds were whistling tree to tree
Their music's message was "Our Southland free!"

A nation once again, my prayer
Like rising mists of morning fair,
An Easter sunrise after rain,
The sun on drops like sweat from pain.

For freedom comes from God's right hand,
And righteous men must stand in band
To break the fetters from off our land
And make a nation once again.

Our bondage over; our agony past,
Now flourish freedom, home, at last.
Our briefest nation, five years dear,
Reborn in light, and our future clear.

Then cherish nation bought with blood,
Fond gift of brave, unselfish, good.
We live to finish what they began
And stand a nation once again.

For freedom comes from God's right hand,
And righteous men must stand in band
To break the fetters from off our land
And be a nation once again,
And be a nation once again.

Beneath The Starry Cross:

A Tribute To Henry Timrod
Sung to the melody of "Galway Bay" (Old Style)

A fair, fair land, our fabled home,
    The South forevermore.
Blue Dixie skies are in our eyes
    From mountains to the shore.

Thank Him who placed us here beneath
    So kind, so kind a sky,
A land of flow'rs forever green
    Beneath the starry cross.

Dyed in the blood of valiant men
    Who gave their lives to be free,
We will remember again, again
    Unfinished work to be.

We celebrate our heritage,
    A goodly one and blessed.
We carry on, our honour pledge
    Beneath the starry cross.

A fair, fair land, our fabled home,
The South forevermore.
Blue Dixie skies are in our eyes
From mountains to the shore.

Thank Him who placed us here beneath
So kind, so kind a sky,
A land of flow'rs forever green
Beneath the starry cross.
A land of flow'rs forever green
Beneath the starry cross.

❖

Revenant At Dawn

I hear the steps,
A careful tread.
I do not leave
My comfy bed.

In semi-drowse
I sleep as drugged.
The curtains move.
I dream a tug.

The toile in swirl;
Is figure real?
When you reveal
A man, not girl.

You turn the corner
Into room
Just inside door frame
Figure looms.

You wear a frock coat
Black cravat,
Your features swarthy,
Wear no hat.

You pause a nonce,
Give knowing glance,
Speak out of curtains,
"You're here at last."

For William Butler Yeats
26 March 1998

I.

The deepest sleep, as deep as inner patines of the blood
That bring forth hidden knowledge
By which our steps are led
In darkest landscapes, tangled maze—
The urge and inclination that's untaught,
The guide unsought
To move the foot to left or right, or go betimes, or stay.
Foot lifts, gives pause, and plants its heel
On soil that's known before.
This is the place of home
Remembered when ourselves are most forgot,
The place of our returning
Forgotten country, found,
Just here around the turn of path,
Discovered bright in dark
When most unsought, forgot.

II.

In time, the baying of the hounds
Will call the crouching body out,
Like dried-up case of chrysalis
From death's own winter bed,
To stretch, unfold, and thaw its marbled limbs
To walk like some numbed walker in his sleep
Or one still hypnotised
To meet the hounds
That come unbidden
Boiling at the feet.
To put on wings to horse's hooves.
We will ride out in hardwood mist
Where silver gray and inky black of branches
Point their fingers like the ink upon the page.
We will ride out on bays and roans and dapples
To the harmony of hounds.
They sing the ballads of our past
So long forgot, but recollected in the blood
And made a past of viscera complete.
Yes, our own deepest natal land
Remembered when we lose ourselves complete
To walk the dim remembered hardwood hills of home.

III.

The days are very first of spring,
The trees have shown no green
But ground now turns expectant bright.
The violet springs beneath the leaf
And year is on the verge.
This is the cusp of knowing,
Of expectations keen,
Of breaking out and through.
The body sinks in saddle
And supples to the gait
Rolling with the sound of hounds and hooves.
The hounds lead on.
Dry wraith of hunter's antique horn
Sounds ghostly in the mist,
Far, far in that forgotten land.

IV.

Yes, Yeats, some day we shall get up before the dawn
And find our ancient hounds before the door,
And wide awake know that the hunt is on.
We lead relentlessly, will or no,
Guided by the voice of hounds in blood
To make genetic certain tie,
Affirm the bond to this our land,
To hear the distant bay
Get ever near
And end with chants of victory
Amid encircling hounds.

❖

THE MASTER OF HAMPTON

He planted hollies as the years unfurled
Green arms outstretched embracing world
And doubled them with dogwoods there
In bloom they mirrored mansion fair.

They came from out the woods around
Their roots returned to native ground.
They stand today a stay to fate
Outside the hour, without a date.

They circle through the spinning years
Alloying time, allaying fears,
Outlasting rulers and their domes
Enriching hearths, endearing homes.

If Time

If time upsets,
Love the poem.
Upset time.

When loved ones go,
Love the poem.
Their eyes are bright.

When petals fall,
Love the poem.
Freshen flower.

If fears of death
Disquiet night,
Love the poem.
Disquiet death.

II.

AGRARIAN POEMS

"Of what is past, is passing, or to come—"

The Happy Isle
(After Horace, Epode xvi)

Here grapes yield fruit without the blade
From tops of trees is honey made.
The figs are dark against the sky
The goats are fat and multiply.
The sheep seek milking paths alone,
Their bells have always merry tone.

This is the happy island blest,
Fair place of peace and silence, rest.
The age of iron all forgot,
The poet guides a happy lot.
Adieu all chaos and despair.
Here live without a fear or care.

❖

Hoc Erat In Votis

This use to be my solemn pray'r
I sang it long
A favourite song:
Vouchsafe a country house, a plot of land
With sprightly spring close-by, at hand;
A bit of woodland would be blessed
Where under trees from plough I'd rest
And let my sheep, my pastures, this and that,
My *all* in fact, except my brain, grow fat.

❖

The "Hercules and Antæus" of Pollaiuolo
In Homage to Allen Tate

Antæus, fable of a first necessity,
Harsh lesson of a sinewed bronze,
Flesh frozen in the forge,
The open mouth agape in pain.
What tongue shall tell your keen outrage?
What living tissue loud proclaim
The strengths that touch the earth always
And act for yours
Jelled in an iron age?
Twin-imaged now we are
Portraying fate of victim, victor same.
Shall we with knowledge carried to the heart
Stand mutely frozen in our shame
To take unacted act to grave?

❖

Message On An Old Chalkboard
To the Memory of John Donald Wade Who Used It Before Me

I.
(1989)

These fine-cut lines of intellect
Have etched here long
A puzzling hieroglyph of closest wisdom.
I mark, therefore, on patterns
Formed before me
Connecting lines to piece the mystery.

Today, and Monticello's sage, for lesson,
Speaks of God's own chosen
To bankers' sons and merchants' daughters—
Of those who till the earth
To those, with any luck, will sell it—
Of nation made of husbandmen
To slick suburbanites
Whose virtues will not grow
In fields and fertile rows.

And as the lines connect
Of fabric delicate,
I trace another hand,
His presence sifts in ghostly chalkdust
Faintest creak of floor.
What marks of yours are these, oh Wade,
The almost vanished,
What tracing to restore?
What fruit of wisdom to be borne
On pavement walked foot-sore?

II.
(2009)

And now the very slates are gone
Are hauled away to fills that scar the land
And you're forgotten long—
A willed amnesia, blind, unkind.

❖

In Memoriam
Andrew Lytle (1902-1995)

The fire he loved to stoke was an image of
his internal energy and gift for conviviality.
—J. O. Tate

No longer will he stand in life
Before his cabin's hearth
The fire of bourbon in his hand.
No longer will the cabin's flame
Heat up the soles of winter pilgrim's feet,
Or brightest talk
Cheer up the weary wanderer's walk.

That fire in memory preserved
Must last in shadow of a cold and much-diminished time,
And heightened in a glowing line
From those so priv'leged in remembering—
Some little solace for a grievous loss.

❖

City Skylines

The fierce green fire
That Leopold beheld
In eye of dying wolf
Will find no place
In mammon tow'rs
That sear all green
From crimson greed
And leave a burned-out land
Of neutral tones—
And daggers to the sky.

Sequoia, pine,
Magnolia, balsam,
Hemlock, beech,
They are the keepers
Of the green
That fall to make
Grey towers rise.
They stand mute tribute
To the wolf's fierce eyes,
Green living ligatures of soil and skies.

NINE-ELEVEN 2001

"The bitter fruits of empire,"
The few wise viewers say
And call them Babel towers
Until they're shouted down.
But those of us with deeper memory
Smell acrid smoke of homes in flame
Across a sabre swath of thousand miles,
And genocidal war of more than hour, more than decades, long.
The mushroom cloud
Of mammon's ticker-tape of litter waste
Wafts like confetti in a street parade
Onto an oily Jersey shore
Like fallout from Hiroshima,
Like cinders from a burning home,
Like ashes from our towns in flame.

The arrogance that seals now-centred eye
And closes selfish ear
Is yet necessity to seal the doom.
"God bless this land!" is yet command, demand, not prayer.
Humility, no jot is there.

"United then we stand!" pathetic phrase
Like paltry talisman
Warding off the days
When brutal empires break like brittle ice
Like twin glass towers splinter,
Fall.

To show man's folly, arrogance, and vice,
A Babel cloud of falling ash,
As fitting emblem, will suffice.

❖

For Dove and Flag, Grandpa Connelly's Mules

I hope Grandfather fed them well
From out his meager store of corn
Or fodder pulled by Mother
'Neath a blazing autumn sun—
So hot sometimes she said that she and sister
Sickened to the vomit stage, and tender arms
Were sliced by leaves' fierce razor edge.

I know they had warm winter barn
And stabled shelter from both heat and cold.
They sometimes got a treat of pea-vine hay
Peanut- or sweetpotato-vines.
Much else but names has come on down
Except their faithfulness of each to each
And to our kin.

No doubt my mother could have told us more
About our two-mule family farm.
But she now too is sadly gone
And with her, recollections of a way of life
So hard and honest as the day was long
And, as she said, the work was never done.

"Your grandpa always dearly loved
To walk behind a mule," my mother said.
And he was faithful still to fought-for soil,
His father's own in days of '65,
Until Depression came in '33
When Dove and Flag were auctioned off
To distant rows and strangers' hands,
With land and house and all.

THE BUTCHERING

Smokes rise in blue-grey scene
Where cauldron boils,
The centre.
Unwilling guest made host
And he there hangs from swingletree
That groans its heavy burden
Of paste-jellied flesh
The centre now.
Entrails smoke and fall
In blue cascade.
Shave cuts ooze, congeal.

How naked to extreme
In death
The all revealed,
And vapor smokes the only shroud.

Dished up to all,
The white flesh falling,
Tasted, eaten, ritual
Of olden days
And death made starkly real
To cherish life
Hug precious
To the breast.

VIDEO SCENE: THE SAME:

Flickers, pixels, frantic skips of dot
Reveal a plastic death
With little loss—
Mirage of death so-called.
Forgotten slain of sidewalks
Soon as sudden
As death and life converge
To blasted eyes.

Miss Ophelia's Garden

What ragged slope is this
In treeless August heat
Beside the two-room cabin perched
All tumble-down!
The slight, bent frame
Grey hair in circled braid
Careful as knot-garden chain
In manor house parterre,
Steps forth Ophelia
Her single simple breakfast done,
To minister with gentle hands,
Made gentler tending tender growing things—
To bring a gullied plot to beauty rare—.
Beside the field-stone chimney,
Zinnias,
Across dirt path vanilla pinks,
By these the baby's breath and ragged robins too
And next her bottle-blues and bach'lor buttons' varied hue.
They onward march in loud display
Of winding paths through broom-swept clay
That's none too good
And only coaxed to life through sixty years
To weave this dazzling tapestry.

Ophelia muses, bending here and there
Her flowered dress of flour sack
Sends back its mirror all around
Like paisley plan
Reflected in a castle pool.

Who is to say
Delight no less than Dante's dream of Beatrice
To summon forth small beauty
From unyielding earth?
Same simple need innate
Fulfilling man's high aim
A beauty to create
That did not breathe before
And far exceeds the joy in what is made.

Ophelia and her quiet smile,
Her shyness asking none,
Tends now her dahlias,—
Florid row, whose stakes
Display the flags of castle court—
Wind-drifted pennons—
Tied for their support.

❖

DROUGHT

I passed your cabin every day,
A grade-school lad
With satchel in the hand.
There wasn't much to look at on the way.
The Johnson grass and new-scraped clay.
But there the slope
With flowers spilling down,
No echoes of the distant town,
Just colours bright in green surprise—
Oases to my thirsting eyes.

The Broken

They limp and drag to August shade
Whatever shade they find,
Broken, bloody, severed leg,
Highway mangled dog.

The hawk stands stunned
With shattered wing
The shot-pierced doe
In covert now to suffer pain.

In aisling dream
They seek a stream,
The broken softly yielding breath
To river wedding life to death.

An Elegy For All Ruined Gardens

Here in dark oaken belt of the forest
Bright vision the new house appeared,
    Palladian frame for the garden
    A conjured levitation endeared.

    Fair-she in blue silken slipper,
    Gentle-he in high riding-boots
They walk orderly twist of the walkway.
    Encouraging each tender shoot.

    No briar to brush of the crinoline,
Fond tendance staying all that impede,
For the path must glide onward in order
    In rhythm of seasons to lead.

Now also in dream, house has vanished
    Bright vision into shadow has passed.
    "Was it ever there?" we ask,
And the paths that so many had laboured
    Their patterns to keep
    Like fair she and he have all faded
Leaving only sharp stones in clay deep.

❖

On He Who Plants The Winter Tree

Old man and young man
Each side they stand
Steadying new-planted tree,
A butterfly's wing.

For young man in spring
With vision of autumns unfolding
Tree fruits on with harvest unending
No thoughts of a tempest to bring.

But old man at end of his season,
No vision of apples to come,
What prompts shaking limbs to embolden
Set spade in the soil he came from?

For young man too filled with his vision
He moves as were he
Had too short a time for a question
Only dreaming of apples to be.

Tree Poem In Winter

Winter limbs
Sail the wind
Like masts of ancient ships;
Dark outline they
Against sea's grey,
Their canvas furled for storm.

❖

A Tribute To Jim Clark

If you live long enough, you may get a poem written about you.
—Old Irish Saying

"Gladly would he lerne and gladly teche" *—Chaucer*

More than friend,
You held the lamp
To show the possibilities of pen,
A fellow trav'ler
In the realms of gold
On pilgrimage
That knows no end.

I honour you in my small way
Of tribute this auspicious day
To pay a debt that's long been due,
Singer, poet, craftsman true.

A friend of old
May be so bold
To speak your name,
Learner, teacher,
gladly same.

We do our part
To say from heart.
A glass we raise
To better days.

❖

Elegy For Tanya Berry's Hillside

(After reading her comments on solar panels in The Need to Be Whole)

"It did not give of bird or bush."
—*Wallace Stevens, "Anecdote of a Jar"*

Sunk seven feet the concrete pylons stand,
To show hard angles to the sun.
Unearthly moonscape now
The product of a new technology.
The husband bit and bought
From out sincerity
But now the panels prove
A sad reality.

"They're just plain ugly," Mrs. Berry said,
"I'll never love them, that's for sure
And have to see them every day"—
And those an ever-shortening few.

A comely shapely hillside
Gone, for sake of human pride,
Belovèd, lovely hillside
Softly dear with curves
Cut deep with manmade knives.
They cut into the retina of eye.
Unearthly logic built them

Cold, devoid of human warmth.
They stand as testament
To human folly one more time;
Replacing old with more machines.
The pylons will not flush with leaves
Nor panels bear a living thing.

Sonnet For Wendell Berry
(After receiving a letter of encouragement)

In world hell-bent on strife
Your poetry and orn'ry self
Have been a highlight of a life
Of warring 'gainst the tide—
Of working (as you say)
On losing side
And making selves at home there.
I heed your kind advice to stand and bear.

Even the old, especially the old
Still need a word that's kind
And I have yours
As you have mine
To keep the furrough straight
The stylus on the line.

❖

Sonnet.
Beyond Wordsworth

The world *is* too much with us!
Well-chosen junk
Weighs heavy on our lives—
A plethora of things
Too much, too many, limits none—
A wonder that a one survives.

The mind, it clutters too—
Words flying off to flinders
Like triggered touch-me-not.

Deep need for silence of the stars
Beyond the noise
An eddying of time
Spring-cleaning of the mind
Emetic of the tyranny of things.

❖

Davis College, Spring 1964

Davis College was the English Department at the University of South Carolina in the 1960s. Dr. Havilah Babcock was department head until his death in December 1964. He was author of *Tales of Quails 'n' Such* and other sporting classics. Davis, surrounded by banks of tall purple azaleas in the 1960s, was replaced by a high-rise tower later in the decade.

Tall windows in the classroom had no screens.
    In spring and summer flung up high
    They let the smell of new-cut grass come in—
        No wall between us and outside.

    Our weekend classes let out short
To world where flowers drooped their purple heads
    And coeds in sun-dresses newly bought
        Showed early blush of sun.

    The hall was open with no doors
    So Babcock's setters had free range.
They came and sniffed us friendly at our desks.
    They brought inside their memories
Of broomsage fields and quails and winter woods.
        Their master smoked too much
        And died in winter of that year.

We junior classmen did not know
But something told us there was loss,
For sadness seemed to hang around
And friendly setters came no more.

A Walk With Michaux At Ballylee
Winter 2018

André Michaux, French botanist to King Louis XVI, came to Charleston in 1786 and stayed a decade. Few have made a more lasting impress on the face of the region in so short a time. He introduced to America the *Camellia japonica*, the tea-olive and tea plant, crepe myrtle, *Firmiana,* chinaberry, gingko, and other flora. He first recorded the native yellow-wood (*Virgilia,* as it was originally called after the poet Virgil), a tree which blooms every third year at Ballylee. The *Quercus michauxii* was named for his son, Francois. The elder Michaux discovered and named the native big-leaf magnolia (*M. macrophylla*), Christmas and broad beech ferns, heart-leaf, flame azalea (*R. calendulaceum*), large-flowered trillium, and many more. He died in Madagascar on another plant-hunting mission. If he was buried, the place is unknown. I like to think he lives on in his plants. Ballylee is the 400 acre plantation in central South Carolina settled in 1783. It has a "Michaux Garden Walk" which features the majority of Michaux's plants along a woodland path. It is the home of the poet, and provides the setting for his poem.

His fragrance greets before his sight
    Fresher than a French cologne.
    It is tea-olive sprays of white,
      Their blossoms seas of foam.
You pass his *Firmiana* bare of leaves;
    Then stands *la reine*—
Japonica in varied shapes and hues.
Your host brought regal lineage to new land.
Chaste winter sunshine lights her lustrous leaves;
    She makes the garden gleam.
"I'm 'specially proud of her," he beams.

Your host's crepe myrtle trunks of ivory
Are skeletons exfoliate—
Bare bones of path's pink powder hues,
A memory of summer sunset eves,
Diviner of a fate that's run,
His bones to bleach in Madagascar's sun.

Then press the gingko's yellow carpet floor.
Next pass swamp chestnut oak *michauxii*—
Broad-chested bearer of host's frame and family name,
The russet bronze of leaves still on the limbs,
A technicolor treat in spring recalled
As mind returns to warmer days and ways,
No chill then on the wind.
Sere leaves set up their chatter as you pass,
Excited tongues in passion of discovery.
You think they have a Gallic lilt.

Across a bridge your host were sure to like
Because of later Frenchman's Giverny design,
You're struck by trunks of ivory in careful line
And scatter of the *macrophylla*'s tattered leaves.
Your host first found it in our Piedmont home.
It stands as arrow-straight as his back-bone.
You pass fine twisted branches of *Virgilia*
He found likewise in treks to Tennessee—

White trunk recalls the panacles of spring.
You recollect its bloom so delicate, so rare.
Third year's the charm, to see her standing there.

Beneath your feet, your host's fair trilliums sleep,
Your path outlined by evergreen of Christmas fern,
His much-loved fav'rite as described by him.
You pass his broad beech fern, heart-leaf, and ladies' fern;
You note the bare *calendulaceum*,
Remember flaming colors of the spring.

Your guide has left you now
At entrance to a darker native wood,
Where inland from far coast
And searching now a distant forest's heart
Wide-eyed encount'ring that unmapped terrain
From which no sail returns.

He's left you tokens of a fond *adieu*.
It is good manners after all
Essential to a Gallic heart;
They richen all your winter walks.
Without them, grievous loss,
And with them, he still stands, remains,
His presence palpable to all.

❖

First Whippoorwill

On this very first night of the spring,
From scuppernong arbour
Dead of leaf,
You are its life
In pulse of song,
Each clearest note,
Ghost leaf in sound.
You people it well
First night of spring;
You cluster with green
Your bower entwined.
First dream,
Then deed,
And the dream, your song,
On this very first night of the spring.

Still Life.
Pavia With Hummingbird.
23 April 2014

The buckeye blooms,
Her beating heart worn on an emerald sleeve
Holding nothing back.
Her horde of sapphires startles forest gloom—
Each jeweled bouquet-spray a whorl of sun-splotched fire.
The winter has been cold,
Her flame thus all the welcome more.

Less chirp than squeak
Electric zap of wings,
Announce the hummingbird is here.
Blossoms nod, bouquet aquiver.
No hurry, we, as if suspended, like the bird
Who's testing, tasting every yellow-throated tube—
Frozen motion like a candle flame.

Still moment this
With world eclipsed
Silencing the standers-by,
Their conversation hushed.
Other birds go quiet—even pileated's jungle cry
And drumming on a trunk.
Hush falls on all.

As suddenly appeared,
Then off bird zips
To fuel quickened life
With nectar's honeyed fire
From honeysuckle's coral red
That's burning bright
In sun-lit tree-top on a distant hill.

Geologists Say

Geologists say
Earth's clay is dust of stars.
That I believe
But not from science chart or learnèd formulae.
Dwarf iris prove it.
Tradescant,
Blue aster and blue gentian too,
Sky-coloured violets
By clearest stream,
Blue birds in new spring coats—
They've brought the heavens down,
Have power to reflect, declare
All origins.

Bounty

Bullace and scuppernong
Wild flavours and perfumes
Important among harvests.
Wild strawberry and low-bush huckleberry.
Perfume of *chionanthus* and sweetshrub,
Better than barter and trade,
Sky-song of geese,
Pattern of butterfly wings, bearing no bar code—
Early remembrance they,
Glad of return
Renewing the mind, in circling year,
Past all beginnings,
Beyond all stars.

❖

Old Farmer Lyman's Maxims For The Modern Time

Better red neck
Than nervous wreck.

Better clod hopper
Than blade dodger.

Better song of the lark
Than shot in the dark.

Better long country furrough
Than city rut in a hurry..

Better greetings that matter
Than office's chatter.

Better life that's not neuter
Than an on-line computer.

Better hand in the soil
Than a freighter of oil.

Better house in the dell
Than prisoner's cell.

Better pancakes and syrup
Than poison of gossip.

Better creaking porch swing
Than a Las Vegas fling.

Better cuffs that are frayed
Than to sleep half afraid.

Better dirt under nails
Than business that fails.

Better fear flood and drought
Than a job that's in doubt.

Better honeybee's honey
Than to lust after money.

Better own well-known tillage
Than vague global village.

Better cedar and pine
Than assembly line.

Better speaking direct
Than psyche that's wrecked.

Better nap in the shade
Than Super-Bowl played.

Better biscuits at dawn
Than cellular phone.

Better bottle in front of me
Than frontal lobotomy.

Better sowing of seed
Than garden of greed.

Better work with your son
Than to meet on the run.

Better biscuits and butter
Than to sleep in the gutter.

Better call of the quail
Than shrill siren and jail.

Better feet on the soil
Than traffic-jam broil.

Better fear of your God
Than an overlord's rod.

Better user than tool
Better farmer than fool.

A Seed Is Memory

A seed is memory
Mutely destined to fulfill, return.
It can be counted on
To be itself
Content to live in universe contained
Within hard bounds.
A seed is patience concentrated down—
Epitome of waiting, essence of itself,
A truth to trust,
Tradition's firmest friend,
Only seeking soil.

❖

Written In The Centre Of A National Forest

Any fool can kill a tree
The tree just stands there—
No hunting skills required.
And even if the tree could move
The fool would chase it down
To bring the crown to ground
So it would lower be
Than fool's own dunce's cap
On dunce's stool—
An equalising act
To satisfy an inward lack
And show the tree who's really boss.

I'd sometimes like to post this forest with big signs
NO CUTTING IN THESE PINES!

City Billboards

As if they didn't already look enough like Wal-Mart shelves,
These city streets
Now even bear their price tags
Lit at night, with flashing arrows.
They shout and jostle,
Shove and shoulder higher
To push their wares
O'er all their rivals,
Ill-mannered hustlers in the crowded walks.
The world while riding through seems now
One giant outdoor rummage sale
With final arrow flashing point:
"Buy *me*. Buy *me*.
I'm grand. I'm cheap.
And I'm on sale."

An Elegy For The Whitmire Pig

Its sign went years
Without its letter **P**
So I shopped at the **iggly Wiggly** store.
Her aisles were tight.
You couldn't meet your neighbours without talk.
There was a quiet buzz
Of conversation hovering o'er
Above the cans of Campbell's and the Bunny Bread.
It had the chitterlings and all the nameless parts
You never bought
But somehow strangely comforting
To know they all were there.
White folk and Black folk joined
Across two checkout lines,
The buggies though they differed
In so many ways
Clanged out the same front door.
You held it open each to each.
No automatic openers for the Pig,
No "Greeters" at the door.

You didn't know you'd miss it when it closed,
So small a part of shopping life, but more.
Communal Pig where mart replaced the church
'Cause neighbours went to more than one.
But Pig was solitary and she reigned supreme.
Her asphalt lot had holes
Could swallow up a truck
But you had learned exactly where they were
And never hit a one.

Sprawl-Mart: A Mock Heroic

You had a trove of catty ugly names
To humanise the place in some strange way—
Wal-Fart and Mexi-Mart
Were but a few.
You'd have to choose according to the company you'd keep.
But they all signified the same,
Because they'd killed the corner store,
Which had in turn killed off
The crossroads crackers and hoop cheese
And pickled eggs in pink that looked
Like they were in formaldehyde.
A wondrous land to enter with your dog
And warm against pot-bellied stove
Where owner's socks hung on a wire to dry
And you could hear the pepper
Of the sleet on its tin roof.
The dogs they came and went
Because there was a tear at bottom of screen door
Conveniently to let inside the crew of dogs and cats,
Who counted on the place to be not-fixed.
Its slam would shake the tins upon the shelves
And ring to rafters that were all exposed,

An honest skeleton like hull of ship
Perhaps a Noah's Ark against some storm to come.
The sound comes back
From gulf of time.

An automatic door
Requires no holding it of courtesy
And cheerful "Thank you. Much obliged,"
With meeting eye to eye.
We've mechanised and merchandised the world,
Denatured it of country stores,
No more accommodating all its creatures great and small.
The world has gone all citified
And country folk have fear
They might be labeled countryfied.
Sprawl-Marts will asphalt-pave the world
And do away with game of checkers,
Well-worn cards.
Instead, will robot-stock the shelves.

But automatic doors may open soon
To empty shelves
And any shelf that's full
Will prove a find.
This is a warning to us all
To eat our backyard chickens country-fried.

❖

The Hidden Wound
23 February 2002

It bleeds beneath its armour,
Buckled eagle-crusted bronze breastplate,
Keeps hidden so it will not heal.
Imperial legions
Press the soil
Their starry banners casting blight and shadow on the land.

The heavy-footed ones
Tramp in formations long and deep.
They do their work
In offices, on screens, classrooms.
They march from pulpits,
News headlines, and corporate boardrooms,
The work of death
Begun so many years before
With conquering feet invading land.

Hidden wound,
Invasion still the word cannot be breathed.
The armor plate still covers all—
Imperial legions holding sway.
Yet moist beneath each petty Caesar's bronze
The sabred wound
Still bleeds.

Swallowtail Summer

August comes on wings
Vinca and the phlox,
Lantana too and four o'clock,
They all can tempt
The Spice's eyes—
Peacocks imaged on the lawn.

Tiger's abstract art
Can sometimes stop the heart.

Zebra needs the pawpaw
And thus is often rare
But when it does appear,
We mark it on the calendar
And wonder where the pawpaws are.

NEEDS

Each time I see a Zebra Swallowtail
I wonder where the pawpaws are.
The Zebra needs the pawpaw,
Which is rare
And we need Zebras by the ton.
Let's level town
To make a pawpaw farm.

Following The Santa Float

Santa rides a sugar mountain peak
Confectioner's delight.
His tinsel is rock-candy on a string.
He sports a whipped-cream beard
As topping to a cherry cobbler suit, that's oozing sweet.
This jolly fat old elf
Is fat indeed!—
Quintessence of all syllabubs
And ultimate kinds of Arctic Dairy ice,
Big Baked-Alaska too
With reindeer like some chocolate rabbits frozen
In mid-leap.

And why it is I follow tall o'er bobbing heads,
Who stops to think?
As caught in rush of scrambling hands
Retrieving silver-covered cubes, I stand and watch in trance
That rivets eye of Santa
At parade's chaotic end,
When with last throw, not handfuls now,
But one lone twisted taffy swirl, —
He aims at diabetic me.

❖

Dream Poem In An Old House

I love the yellow beetles in the wall
I hear them scratch though they are small
Companions only in this time of need
Though I've not seen them, messages I heed.
I love the yellow beetles in the wall.

I love the yellow beetles in the wall
Antennae twitch, I hear them call
Their lonely midnight life they do not share
Skull-shaped they are but do not scare.
I love the yellow beetles in the wall.

I love the yellow beetles in the wall.
They've never seen the sun at all.
They burrow on some lonely chore
Inside the wall, beneath the floor.
I love the yellow beetles in the wall.

I love the yellow beetles in the wall
Scarabs rare and scarabs kind
Inhabit corners of the midnight mind
Blind to the world they did not make
They find old wood's their piece of cake.
I love the yellow beetles in the wall!

❖

Golden Girl

Yellow braids aglow
I chance to see you there on campus lawn
Half-hidden by a van
Beside the parking lot,
A fleeting vision out of drear,
Beneath the yellow tree
Whose leaves
Half on,
Half off the tree
Fill up the world with gold.

What stroke of luck
That you put on today
Your brightest yellow dress
And brought, unknown,
This sunlight to my day
Full filled with golden leaves
That matched your golden braids.

❖

The Teacher Observes His Students During An Exam

The young ones at their desks
    Exhibit many scars.
    On one a lighter line
Along the ball of wrist well-browned,
    He, the sturdy athlete.

Beside him raw new scrape
On dainty upper arm blue-bruised.
    So long it is, you wonder
If performed in order just to pain,
    And painful now to see.

All hold our wounds to light
    For all the world to see—
    Inflicted from without,
With hope, healed from within.

Puritan

To love your God with all your soul
And neighbour hate with all your heart
Is dire abstraction's curse,
The second thus denying first.
The two must always present be
Or bells will have no honesty to ear
And broadcast hollowness, hypocrisy
A fatal curse to all who hear.

Doggeril I.
Musings On A Pseudo-Southern Bard

What tragedy is this
To live to be so old
And not be whole
Because there is a hidden wound
From conflict of a homeless kind
That leads to live a lie.

So sad to be deprived
Of your own people and their honest toil
Berated, pilloried, despised—
To be like some still-infant brat that's spoiled
And seeks to shame a loving sire
For giving him his all.

Gary Snyder will not do
As surrogate for pater true.
You need a grandsire too.
You had them if you knew—
Achieved with no or little pain.
To Californicate a life for gain
Is more than pitiful, is shame
And only for Establishment acclaim
Within its slimey walls.
It only shows you have no brains
And worse than that, no balls.

Doggeril II.
The Same Subject (In A Moment Of Pique)

What tragedy is this
Near ninety years to live a lie
To make career of rootedness in place
And be without a tie
To your own writing people
Willfully denied.
What shame, what shame
To be in letters rootless
And without a home.
No matter that you till the native soil,
The soil is only foil
To those who tend'st and now have done.
What shame to live in literary tent
Like Bedouin on barren sands
Rejecting what your culture still demands.
A tear for you
The homeless, fatherless,
An orphan bounced upon a stranger's knee,
Your blood denied
And now for all the world to see.

❖

Homage To Ezra Pound.
War Protest, Athens, Georgia, February 2003

I sit beneath the arch with sign at feet,
LISTEN TO THE PEOPLE scrawled letters say
And I with lesson to prepare for morrow's day
Hugh Selwyn Mauberley to read,
And heed that same blind toothless hound
Howling dying in her cave
That battered hundred books to save
And plaster art made by the gross.

This is a Southern land
And worth the saving sure.
Our art is in our lives and in our hearts
And reaches to the page, to canvas, keys, and strings.
We live our lives as tales of kith and kin.
We know the worth we have.

Friend Pound,
I wish you'd known our Southern land.
With you today.
We'd make another stand.

The monkey cage might wait us all
For challenging a monster's cell,
But we would singing gladly go
To gulag's icy bars—
Better than the bloody ones—
And bristling razored, dagger-pointed stars
On Empire's bleeding rag.

❖

Cage Country
(In Memory of James Dickey)

For those who find their comfort in the cage
 They've made a peace with inches.
Their narrowed eyes are taught to gaze
 No further than the finches.

Instead, adjusted to the square,
 They turn to inward seeing.
They never look beyond the grill
 Or ever think of fleeing.

They cozy to their dwarfed domain
 Allowing only not to do.
They have no vistas to the sun
And spurn the likes of me and you.

War Protest II, March 2003

I watch as thrashing beast
Bleeds out its ghastly blood.
**NO BLOOD FOR OIL,
SAY NO TO EMPIRE,
WHO WOULD JESUS BOMB?**
The signs emblazoned read.
Imperial legions press the desert sand.
Depression stalks the markets of a hardened land.
Protestors grow in lengthening lines,
Trillioned deficit mushrooms
Like cloud above Hiroshima sublimed.
Empire implodes
Collapses on its bloated paunch
Like dying Muslim, doubled,
Decapitate with sword.

We watch beneath a Southern arch of old,
WISDOM, JUSTICE, MODERATION,
Its classic motto reads.
Around, before, the dying beast
Bleeds out imperial lie.
It flails about, destroying all within its sphere
And will not wisely go.

❖

III.

CHAUNCEY'S POEMS
OLD AND NEW

Druid Poem

The tree is king
The woods resound in everything.
The standing stone is fine
But does not match the pine.

The ash o'er it holds sway,
It reigns to mark the day.
In hieroglyphs they march
When all is put to torch.

Grey beards they shine like beechen bark
Wise heads, they teach in utter dark
Their chants record in stone
Tree soldiers etched with bone

The tree alone is king
The woods resound in everything.

Chauncey Reflects On His Verse

Moments crystalised:
The flow and stop of time,
The history of me
And of my kind.

Chauncey Pays Tribute To His Laurel Tree

You ringed the brow of conqueror—
Athlete the same
(Your green against the golden curl
And now that curl in dust).
You crowned the deep-browed bard,
Whose leaves do rival only
Lasting green.

Chauncey Envisions A Fire-Tree

Anchored at fireside
In ashes of own death, dancing the flame
Of glow-hearth spread-veined splay of root,
You take your leave
Through chimney trunk
To leaf anew in crystal bell black night winter of stars:
Soul of all-trees
Given in homage to warmth,
Sacrifice splendid,
Resurrecting in weave of a night-realm dance
To music of spheres, re-created.

❖

RHYMES FOR THE OLD MEN WHO PLANT TREES

Society great grows, the proverb goes,
When old plant trees and fully know
They'll never sit in shade below.
It's harder then to lift the spade
And wobbly knees make half afraid
They'll topple in the holes they've made.

But plant they do when hopes are few
Just like Candide who worked indeed
To tend some soil with honest toil
Outside whose gates the crowd in moil
For prey awaits and life abates.
They'll stay inside. They have their pride.

These men are planted at the last.
Their names are lost, their stories past.
The trees grow tall, confronting all.
Their bark is rough, their branches tough,
Surviving then, triumph enough.

❖

OLD HOUSE

(For Adam Nicolson Whose Image I Use)

I shrugged on this place like a heavy old coat
    By decades of coat-hook pre-formed.
    Coat on, tackled boarded-up porch
    Big hole in the roof, columns prone.

    Stones testified places that were,
    Traces of sheds, vanished old barns
    Briar woods blurring old garden lines
    Thickest tangle of privet and vines
Centuried garden dissolved by the pines
    And the thorn.

    But the farm kept its form
    To trace and behold.
Whispered voices and shadows cajoled,
Revenant gifts clear guiding the way,
    Lighting the night
    Cats' eyes in the dark.
Remembered distinct in the day.

❖

Summer Morning Dawns On The Plantation

Throw wide the flowered curtains
And pin them to their stays.
The orange bristling ball
Peeps o'er the woodland wall
And sings upon the boxwood lanes
And on the river bottom canes.
The air is cool and fresh on lawn
At new creation's early dawn.

Chauncey Longs For Home In Spring

I know the phoebe builds above the door,
The wren investigates a place to nest once more,
A dappled dove will sit and preen
At dusk without the window screen
And just beyond the window's light
At lantern-lighting time,
It is the hour of whippoorwill,
The first I know
Is chorusing from distant hill.

I travel home in mind
Beyond an asphalt odyssey unkind.
Against a time I'll make return
The hands of clock stand still.
'Til then, I make an inner place
To pleach a nest of memory
To stand against the wind and rain.
I've seen the house birds do the same.
They take the refuse of a city scene
In stalwart beak, a scrap and tuft a time,
Beneath the diamond eye.

I long for Ithaka beloved,
Far down Ægeans of the mind
To live again with dead and yet unborn
Beyond the foreign window sills
In folds of gentle far-off hills.

Chauncey's Spring Song For An Old House

My candle burns within its crystal bell.
It makes the shadows dance,
Projecting sprays of sarvis,
Drifts of silverbell—
Patterned lace
Upon the parlour wall.

❖

Chauncey Remembers

They come reflections of a far-off day—
The darting deer too shy to stay,
Two rows of jonquils made to form a path
Down which my silent youth has stepped away.

Mutability

Images from the past
When least expected come
The clustered snow drops at the gate
In yard so bare of all but clay,
The shining roofs of tin in rain,
The darting deer too shy to stay,
Two rows of jonquils
Made to form a path
Down which my silent youth
Has stepped away.

❖

Winter Solstice

The year is dead.
The sun skulks at horizon's line.
It cannot lift its weary head
To meet you as you walk
With axe on back
And boots made heavy
From the day.

I do not know
The winter's depths
But glimpses have
In monotone grey sky,
Bare limbs in black,
The wind among the seed pods
Of the weeds,
Dry and rattling,
Stoic in the cold.

Like shooting stars
Cold raindrops shine
Against an ink-dark sky.

The robins lift in unison,
They circle in wet cedar grove
With gentling and unhurried cry.
They move on swiftly
But without alarm.

Lost In The Thorny Wood

My tangles lead me none
And foot tripped ties hold firm.
Pierce briar and the limb-lash keep.
Vine fetter fall and fold,
Trap net and web,
Of mind-twist branch-bar
Freeing none.

Axe longing
We fail.

❖

Full Christmas Moon

Neighbours are cajoled to open doors,
Enchanted from their walls
To stride blue-shadowed walks.
Eyes cannot look away
From heavy circle of departing year.

Entire landscape leans and yearns
With farm's own free-range brood
Line topmost limbs of cedar tree,
They look like row of ditto marks precise
Their heads all face in mirrored same
The magnet moon.

With pea-brain small, in light of day,
They cannot find their way through fence,
Or think to fly above.
But here they sit
With proper reverence,
Like congregation, rapt, intent,
Or chastened children in a row at school,
Expectant half, like all who see
This heavy circle of a year.

What must their pea-brains think?
Perhaps they don't
And only bask in light of orb,
Attracted in the sway
Like tides.

Like unborn in the swelling belly yet,
We all yearn to the Christmas moon.
Light of life come down to earth
To save from dark, eternal death.

Chauncey's Song

The seasons' rhythm is a song.
Leaves fall
To prompt the buds to bloom.
By such, we count the metre of our days.
Day and night,
Sunrise and set
Are but a rhyme.
The generations link into an epic's tune.
We plough a set of rows,
A couplet neat
And turn to plough two more again
To form a quatrain mirroring the year.
The lines of verse or soil
But turn and prance to cosmic dance.

The fertile pairing man and wife
But parses out the song of life.
Habits, features, faces,
Gestures of our kin
Wherein they rise again
Alliterate to grand processional.

And life whose age in folding
Back to bud to bloom again
Is universal metric pulse of life.
The finger on the vein
Can tell all time,
The metronome to keep us on our way.

We walk an early path,
Retrace our steps at end of day,
And make a dance across the years.

The years themselves
Repeat themselves,
And all our duty is to sing,
And parse the line
With song the sign
Of oneness with the world.
We chant our song
With bards among,
Of what is past or passing and to come.

❖

Chauncey Sees His First Cranesbill In His Winter Woods

Eyes with winter weary,
Downcast with cold,
See pink among the dun.
It's cranesbill's pink
And flower's first,
Raised high on spindly stem alone,
Like kerchiefed head on craning neck
To turn in breeeze,
Look this, then that,
Seeking after sun.

The cranesbill wakes
And brings surprise of spring
Full-blown.
"She's here. She's here!"
The winter-weary chime—
Full-blown and pink
With head raised high,
And searching after sun.

❖

Rain In March

Robins call to punctuate,
Whispers sibilant of rain.
Lenten lilies droop with wet.
A raucous crow flies over scene.
The blue of roman hyacinth
Reminds the blue of sky
Forgotten since in days of rain.

The world has turned to shallow sea,
With greening grass between the waves.
The Quaker Ladies seem to float
Like Noahs in their floods.
Dripping cedars hang branches low
And mud collects on violets.

Your tennis shoes will stand no chance,
Wet socks are up to dry,
And you stay in
To watch the world
Through glass
With slower eye.

❖

Persimmon Fall

The time of Flicka's feast—
Grey-speckled backs
Race up and down
On bark that looks like theirs.

They shake their choosy heads,
Inspect,
Rejecting this or that,
And sharpen beaks.

Fat orange fruits
Hang all around
Among the purpling leaves
Against the sky of sea.

In The Short Rows.
Chauncey's Poem On His Fortieth Birthday

Two-thirds through man's three-score-ten
Rows are shorter
Start to blend
With far horizon,
Distant trees.

The jug of tea
Is in the shade.
The fiddle waits
For songs long played.

The mule is tired.
And so are we
Ham-biscuits wait
Beneath the tree.

Short rows give time
To relish prime
To sit beside the fire
And doze.

To tell the tales
Without the ends
To narrate circling to the friends
And with no rush to close.

Chauncey In Praise of Writer's Block

When rhymes don't come
The mind can rest.
Rhymes take away the peace
And make you pace.
Sometimes the brain must lull
Into a single monotone,
The hum of going deaf
Or distant highway's drone,
The snow of TV sign-off in the night.
Sometimes the mind must vegetate,
And make no sound,
Grow sloppy fat from lack of exercise,
Eat M&Ms
And brownies by the pound,
Drink heavy cream in coffee
Munch doughnuts by the mound.

The diet of a rhyme,
A clean-turned line
Are like the extra workout set
Or added mile.

I do not want them now,
When sprawling at his ease
Affixed to lounge chair in the den
The little music man inside
(Except for snore)
Is silent for the time,
His cheeks puffed out
With custards, cakes, and pies

❖

Chauncey Observes His Pumpkin Vines In June

As days do strain for longer sun
And earth yearns toward a solstice noon,
So do my pumpkin vines in June.
They wrap their chartreuse tendrils as they go
Against the summer's shocks and storms.
Their flowers are too bright for fall
With winter on the wind;
They're summer flowers after all
That image forth a waxing sun
With heated bees' activity o'ermuch
"Making hay as ol' Sol shines," as saying goes of old.
The bees are gilded with the flowers' gold.
No fruit as yet weights down the vine;
The juices flow as yet to rambling and to green
Like all the young in early leaf.
Each day they've grown a foot at least, I'd swear
Rambunctious, splurging out, as sun climbs high
And grown to paths unknown before.

Their limber stems are wondrous malleable;
They'll curl and drape
And double back
For teaching where they'll not be tread upon.
Mere breeze can change their course—
That is, before the tendrils take
And anchor to a chosen spot on earth.

Past Solstice and the fruits set on,
Will venture heavy forth so little then,
So plump complacent fleshy sure,
They'll be content to sit and soak
Last ray of autumn sun—
The heavy orange disk of sun themselves they are—
Round orange bellies now on chilling ground
Amongst the dwindled stems whose leaves are none
In browning world around.

❖

The Times.
Chauncey Vents To A Friend

I've had my fill of sanctimoniousness—
The dripping honey gone to mead turned black.
Much talk of honour, loyalty,
By those who leave the dagger in the back.

I will not blame them overmuch
They're but a product of their day
A time they say is better than the past
But pompous, selfish they—among the worst of worst.

It is a hapless, hopeless age
Misled by those who slew their past
And dashed the classic urn to shards
Replaced by tins as roadside trash.

⌘

Chauncey To His Books

My fathers are content to wait my time
To sit with them and parse their lines,
To trace their words when walking in the world.
I come to them; they cannot come to me.
My mothers likewise keep the hearth
Where hearts can gather to unfurl
And silence speaks without the words.

The fathers and the mothers of our choice.
We choose our parents certainly,
Choice here, discrimination there.
They do not shout to hail us,
Speak only through ourselves,
And anchor us in place
From off our shelves
Around which universes spin.

❖

Chauncey To His Stray

A country dog that's thrown away
Adopts a place because it has no dog.
The place needs dog
As sure as dog's own need.
A farmhouse needs a dog
And dog knows that as well as we
So in comes Staggering Nameless—
A rack of bones that's deep in years and dire in need
Without an empty yard
Or set of steps to guard.
For master of the place
(His master if he heed)
Another mouth to feed
But knows he will give dog a break
At last go forth with crust of bread,
And finally share his steak.

The Countryman's Song At Summer Dawn
In memory of A. E. Housman

Hurry to greet the sun
In cool of summer day,
For morning sun will run
And hours race away.

Throw wide the flowered curtains
And pin them to their stays.
Be up and at it Bozo;
This is no time to play.

The Ploughman's Reverie

The furrough is a perfect place for reverie
No better place to plant life's dream
Or understanding of its worth
In cleaving of the earth.

The ploughman plants his reverie
And tills it under new-turned loam
To flower with the aid of providence
A providential hope of home.

Gardenias In Bloom

A single branch holds history
Of things that pass
And things abide.
Quick flowers flesh-like, fleeting, fading, frail
With which our finite minds can halfway deal—
We as the dust from off a midnight moth's grey wing;—

But leaves that last in winter blast
In shining green and do not fail
Are spirit riddles past the night
And past the spring
Beyond all finite minds of men.

Chauncey Casts His Pearls.
A Variation Of Matthew 7

He ventured growing piglets dear.
It was a chore, I think,
But pigs with wrinkled nose in pink
Could laugh him into tears.
Thus oinks became endeared.

He said:
"When I want audience for verse
And oinking criticism terse
I have but just to go to pen
And gauge their beady eyes perverse.

"King James doth warn that they will rend
But these my loyal dears, defend;
They do not trample like my piers.
They're use to laughter, jeers, and slop
And viewing rears, curled tails atop.
They oink me eager: *Do not stop!*"

Chauncey's Rendering
From The Seventh Century Gælic

Grant me the grace to find—
Son of the living God—
Sod that's fertile, seasoned home
To make it my abode.

Crystal river, silent, deep
To flow beside the place,
To wash my sins, refresh my soul
By sanctifying grace.

Deepest woodlands circling,
Shielding winter wind,
Twining branches for the birds,
Before it and behind.

And all I ask of housekeeping—
I get and pay no fees,
Peas from garden, poultry, game,
Perch and bream and bees.

My share of clothing and of food,
From Lord of fairest face,
Gift to sit at times alone
And pray in every place.

Chauncey's Inscription For His Wood

Here poet Chauncey girdled pines
To make a forest without lines.
The lines he made with father's plough
And with his pen in rhymes set down.

May woods full grown vouchsafe you peace
Its oaks and ashes, poplars, beech,
The blessings of strong life and calm,
On banks of fern to find fit balm.

If any Chauncey seek in after times
Must search within his woods and lines.

IV.

AIRLIFT

In Praise of The Romantics

Adonais they and he, as Shelley knew,
The one remains, the many change and go.
Oh Adonais, flesh consumed,
Eyes fever staring, shining bright
Beyond the many-coloured dome of earth
To blinding whiteness through the fire of life refined
All burned away—the passions, griefs,
The joys, beliefs,
All aspirations young,
All dross before refining fires consumed
With treasured residue the words
True etched with stylus sharper than engraver's tool
Beyond a jeweller's skill
Or chisel on the stone
As hard as diamond from the coal.

THIS HAND
(A Lenten Meditation)

This hand
That holds the pen
Holds ash,–
Burned Lenten branch,
To mark the brow,
Reminding flesh.

These ropes of form
That trace the shape
Of shadows
Cry cinders,
Reminding flesh.

This hand, in crease,
Shows largest letter
Of Mortality,
Initial carried from our birth
Reminding flesh.

It is the place
The nail went in
To promise life within the M
We're bought with price
Of sacrifice
Reminding flesh.

❖

Airlift

(From out the helicopter)

The woods they change to farms,
Farms into city streets;
It is the progress of a place
To placelessness.

An ethered flight
Man wrought.
But risen into death
And coming back
Rejoicing to the light.

The fateful pang
To flower
Into thankfulness
Renewal daily marvelling
At a heightened world.

What Wonder Of A Year

What wonder of a year!
That goes beyond three score and ten
For salvaged from the dark and into light
Comes down to screen of black and white
Whose featured star's a vital knot.

Life's but a spasm of a sort,
A soldierly contraction short,
A spurt of life
Relaxed in death
Repeated in the rhythmed breath
And God's unfailing metronome.

The Patient Watches His Heart On Ultrasound

A marvel that!
To watch on screen
Your heart in its contractions bold.
Both you,
The nurse, and surgeon too.
They see exactly what you do.

Screen people now,
The image comforts for a time
And seems more real
Than all reality.

Enough of that!
There are some things a mortal should not see.
I turn my face away
And live to face another day.

❖

Long View

In the emergency room
Panic asks,
Will she die? Will he die?
Old doc, he's been around,
World weary now enough
And probably dead-tired—
The emergency was not so dire after all—
Not today he solemnly replies
And with no hint of smile.

Paradox

(In memory of my grandmother Connelly)

Silver coffin cloth
Of silver day
A silver tree in shadow
Silver cross in ash.
Brutal beauty death:
Of day's brocade
In fine-stitched gold
Removed for wetting clay.

Carpet's Figure

What wrought the looms of Hammedan
For wool moth on its way
Across a jewelled splendour?
The brighting wave to glitter large
Eye-shocked piece-on-piece what marvel this!

And we to know also
In path that's monochrome
Toward chrysalis,
When only wing-revealed
Shines forth
The masterpiece.

Lines In Winter.

Delicate the day, she steals
Peering through shutters of night.
Delicate the day, she heals,
Night's shadows dissolved in light.

Delicate the day with life
Promise of hours to come,
Delicate the day with hope
Hushing the memories of strife.

Delicate the day, she sets
Passing through each tint of grey
Delicate the day, she rests,
Breath and pulse to stay.

Delicate the day's last gleam,
Faded to restful ease.
Delicate the day is done,
Red curtains across the sun.

Written In The Year 2021
(Recalling Micah, VI)

Beware the pitiless gaze
Of times that bear no mercy.
Seek no justice, truth.

Beware sharp arrow set to string
For prouder game.

When truth and mercy sleep,
Be sure they be not dead.

❖

December Song

"Who sings prays twice,"
They say you'd hear Augustine say
On rocky hill-top far away.
Tonight full wafer of a moon arose
From out the east
To silver boxwood rows,
Its white against the winter cold.

The Southern nightingale
Augustine never knew from his stronghold
But if he'd heard her song this night,
A trilling without stop for minutes long,
He'd understood her prayer there in the dark
And surely prayed along.

'Twas more than joyful and full-throated ease
To sing of summer in the plaintive dark,
Though that is right—Notes had a holy edge
Anticipating birth of Saviour to the world—
A pity that so many more could heard—

But with these lines return a chorale there
To sing paired memory and tribute fair.

❖

September Song.
In Praise Of The Well-Worn Path

I walk on paths set down before me
Follow feet I do not know
Design resigned does not confine
Unknowing steps the way I go.

The way I go laid out before me
Travelled, worn in impressed clay
No burden felt, it lightly draws me
From rise of sun, to set of day.

The footsteps many, oft-times repeated
A-down the echoed avenues of time
They channel needs and wants receded
They echo in the family line.

To rise again they submerge feeling
Sublime the impulse, curb the veer
They keep on track to destination
Laid out before for many a year.

These gentlest chains, they do not fetter
Turn velvet, silken at the last.
The guide that welcomes to hereafter
No land that's strange on well-worn path.

To sink in soil that's not forsaken
Well-worn, well-known and friendly home
No thing to fear or ever ponder
No wonder puzzling to its own.

❖

James Everett Kibler, Jr.

Plough Monday.
Yorkshire, UK, 8 January 2024

"Godspeed the plough," we dance and sing
In homage to our new-crowned king,
At Highgrove he's a farmer,
For all th'Organics, a charmer.

Our song restates remembered truths
Of eating ham and lamb and fruits
The produce of our own-o
Of seeds that's sown
Of fleece that's shorn
And then that's worn
Fed from our grass on the lawn-o.

We shear the wool, then wear it
We lift the load, then bear it.
By ploughing deep and sowing
By reaping neat and mowing,
The larder's stored
For bounteous board,
No wonder that we're never bored.

We know were it not for our seeding
There'd be but some very poor feeding.
We're sure you would else starve without it
So with friends 'round us now
Sing Godspeed the plough;
Long life and success to the farmer.

Wearing white for the day
Our own music we'll play.
We're deaf to the distant chime-o
For there all their poets don't rhyme-o.
They've fallen away
So here we will stay
Their books on the shelf,
We'll take care of ourself.

As the pints go around
Here's a toast to our ground.
Long life and success to the farmer!

Hallowed

Her hills were battlefields
Her sons lie in the sod,
Her sunset creeks still colour red
The heart's-blood of remembered dead.
For sake of them, we gently tread.

Then softly, gently tread the soil
The sacred soil of sacrifice
The soil made holy with their toil
The soil made sacred with their strife.

Tread softly, gently on the soil
The hallowed soil of tears and loss
The hallowed soil reclaimed from spoil
Of fearsome hate-filled hordes that crossed.

Tread softly, gently on its dead
Their dust enriches with each year.
Be conscious of the soil you tread
Its purchase came with many a tear,

Our land beloved of sacrifice
Of those who passed the fire to you
Will pass true title etched in life
To those who keep the story true.

True sons and daughters ever own
Remembered sacred soil today
The treasured soil to them on loan
No matter what the deed books say.

These are true owners of the place
True keepers of the fabled land
Who to the future turn the face
And know whereon they firmly stand.

Fair Southern Land
To the Tune of "Steal Away"

Southern skies, summer nights
Our Dixie homeland dearest.
The days unfold, the years pass by
Still she abides, endures it.

I.

We'll stay by her, our mother fond.
She is a royal lady.
Her thirteen sons, with stolen fields
Must now reclaim their homeland.
Chorus (first stanza above)

II.

Her enemies pronounce her dead,
They've wanted it so dearly
But she holds on, and will as long
As sons and daughters will it.
Chorus.

III.

We know we have a right to be
To be ourselves so clearly,
So we have claimed a place on earth,
For our fair land, a new birth.
Chorus

IV.

Her vallies mined, her forests bared
We hold to heart, restore them.
What we stand for, we stand upon.
We'll now take back our homeland.
Chorus

V.

We"ll stay by her, our Mother fond.
She is a royal beauty.
Her thirteen sons, with stolen fields
Must now reclaim their homeland.
Chorus

27 July 2008, 24 June 2024.

❖

Dixie Battle Hymn
To the tune of "Mo Ghile Mear"

Solo: *Deo vindice* we pray,
Deo vindice each day.
Gather round our hearths to say,
We beg Thy blessing on our cause.

Trio: Blood that flowed on Shiloh's hill,
Point Look Out, Elmira's hell.
Chickamauga's reddest field,
Our blood-encrimsoned greenest dell.

All: Bodies piled in Devil's Den,
Bodies heaped in unmarked sod,
Soldiers looking to our God,
Their dying breaths beseeching Him
Deo vindice we pray,
Deo vindice each day.
Gather round our hearths to say,
We beg Thy blessing on our cause.

Trio: They gave their all so we might stand
On native land, our rights demand
Freedom of our dear scorched soil
And back from vandals take the spoil.

All: Their bravery and right we share,
Their heritage of fight we bear—
Brave men who shed their blood in care,
So we may stand their flags to bear.
Deo vindice we pray,
Deo vindice each day.
Gather round our hearths to say,
We beg Thy blessing on our cause.

Trio: So we will carry on their fight
So steeled in faith and mailed in right.
So we will meet the challenge straight
To conquer ill and vanquish hate.

All: Bold principles for which contend
We gallantly proclaim again,
In our own time for Liberty
Forged by their deeds and chivalry.
Deo vindice we pray,
Deo vindice each day.
Gather round our hearths to say,
We beg Thy blessing on our cause.

Trio: And we will free our long held soil
And we for Freedom ever toil
And we will free our homeland dear—
Our people free from cells of fear.

All: Now we will break the captor's chains,
Now loose his mind-forged manacles,
Now cleanse our land from all his stains,
And shout victorious sea to hills.
Deo vindice we pray,
Deo vindice each day.
Gather round our hearths to say,
We beg Thy blessing on our cause.
Deo vindice we pray,
Deo vindice each day.
Gather round our hearths to say,
We beg Thy blessing on our cause.

2008

DEEP SOUTHERN SUMMER
WRITTEN AT MIDNIGHT

Remember.
This is a fought-for land
There's blood soaked in the soil.
There's tears within its waves
And wails upon the shore
Its tempests veil the shrieks
Still heard from years of yore.
There's terror in its shades
Dark places in its woods recall
Much pain unthinkable.
The pain must still remain
It cannot sublimate so soon.
The prayers of victims stay.
They do not die away.

Remember.
This is a fought-for land.
There's blood soaked in the soil.
There's terror in its shades
Heart-breaks unthinkable.

❖

The Land Remains

Proud families bow
Their lineage fails
Before the oak.
The land prevails.

The oak goes down
Its crown to ground
Its limbs make dust.
The land stays sound.

Great castles fall
The mortar fails
Their stones decay
The land prevails.

The roof-tree spoils
Grand mansion fails
It tumbles down.
The land prevails.

Great cities fall
The people gone.
The street grows thorns.
The land lives on.

Tall towers bend
Strong cables break
The grids all fail.
The land prevails.

The domes collapse
Their leaders pass.
They rust to dust.
The land will last.

The steeples fall
No bells to peal
The silence reigns.
The land prevails.

The voices fade
The vellum stains
The poem ends.
The land remains.

James Everett Kibler, Jr.

And The Poem Goes On
In Memory of Fred Chappell, 10 January 2024

You tapped your pint of it
But it flowed on.
You sang your notes of it
But the song sang on.
Your head bobbed up
But now's washed on.
Your silence shouts
But the song sings on.

Deep deep it flows
Is heard in dream
And so it goes
Is seldom seen.
You saw and heard
You hear no more
Your notes now sound
From distant shore.

'Ere long, 'ere long
You're one with song
That's fifty fathoms deep
There sings Ole Fred
We all had known
With the poets at his feet.

Southern Poets Sing Your Songs
(After Yeats)

Southern poets sing your songs
Of Southern life and Southern good
Freedom's blessing— brotherhood,
Standing where the patriot stood.
Southern poets learn your trade.
Sing what is true, what is well-made.
Of purest gold and silver make,
Lines from out our granite take.
Sing out the story of our land,
Squire, yeoman, gentleman,
Fires of ruin, phoenix bright,
Redeemed from out the lucifer light.
From four heroic centuries
Craft out the verse—*We are, will be.*
Our freedom's honest banner see,
So yet and ever, years to be,
Remain the indomitable Southronry.

❖

Good Friday

Behold the Pascal Lamb
Outstretched on hatred's tree,
Love's willing victim sacrificed
For likes of you and me.

We spike him there 'most every day
With acts of greed and enmity
The impulse to destroy and maim
Man's fearful legacy.

Easter Prayer

The light from out the East
Announces joyous feast,
The glooms of shame and loss
Dispelled by light of cross.

It is the day of Grace
Made sacred by Thy face.
Be with us in our pain
Thy crown of thorns to gain.

Illuminate our days,
Thy golden rays to praise,
Make holy with Thy sight
And bless us with Thy light.

LAND OF SONG
Lyrics Waiting for a Tune

When times were hard and news all bad
A head full of rhymes was all we had.
Songs that were barred but we made our own.
Songs we sometimes sang alone.
Our South's been singing for a long long time
And if we were the poets, She was the rhyme.
'Twas our own music that kept us strong
And if ever the singer, She was the song.

Decade after decade, year after year
Season after season, She's still here
And like Her dead, yet still we know
We'll go out singing when we go.
Five-string banjo, a fiddle and guitar
Are some of the reasons we still are.
Singing like then and we always will
Knowing the circle is unbroken still.

Voices raised in harmony
Awaiting day we will be free.
Some voices now are dead and gone.
I'm glad to see you soldier on,
Remembering the songs that pulled us through.
When I hear those songs I think of you.

So thank you for the company.
The music was as sweet as the South's sunshine
Thanks for the company
Thanks for the harmony
I'm here to say the honour was all mine.

30 June 2024

❖

Spring Canticle

He that guides the lark aright
He that manages its flight
He that spreads the heron's wings
He that makes its cries to ring
He that causes leaves to fall
He that spreads the light o'er all
He that makes the willows sway
He that wipes the tears away
He that summons birds to sing
He that blooms the flow'rs in spring
He that makes late snow to fall
He that blankets with the pall
He that shines the silver day
He that makes the breath to stay
He that softly soothes with dark
He that fills the empty heart
He that makes the heart to beat
He that makes the rhymes repeat
Guide us safely, gentle Master
Heed the needy as we go.

❖

First Poem

"Now I lay me down to sleep.
I pray the Lord my soul to keep.
If I should die before I wake,
I pray the Lord my soul to take."

First rhyme remembered when a child
    Petitioning a Father mild.
  It all starts here to have no fear.
  The song begins and never ends.
    It sings beyond the stone.

About the Author

JAMES KIBLER was born in Prosperity, South Carolina and graduated from the University of South Carolina with a Ph.D. in English. His interests have lead him to write on diverse subjects, from botany and agriculture to architecture and art. As a literary man, he has written in several genres, including the novel, short story, and poetry. The history and saga of the renovation of his plantation house is chronicled in his critically acclaimed *Our Fathers' Fields*, which was awarded the prestigious Fellowship of Southern Writers Award for Nonfiction.

It is rare for a writer to excel as both a creative artist and a scholar, but Kibler has achieved such distinction. For many years he was Professor of English at the University of Georgia, he has written authoritatively on many aspects of Southern literature. As a scholar, Kibler is largely responsible for the contemporary rise of William Gilmore Simms studies. He is the founding editor of *Simms Review*, author of the definitive work on Simms's poetry, and the discoverer of many previously unknown Simms writings.

Available From Green Altar Books

If you enjoyed this book, perhaps some of our other titles will pique your interest. The following titles are now available for your reading pleasure… Enjoy!

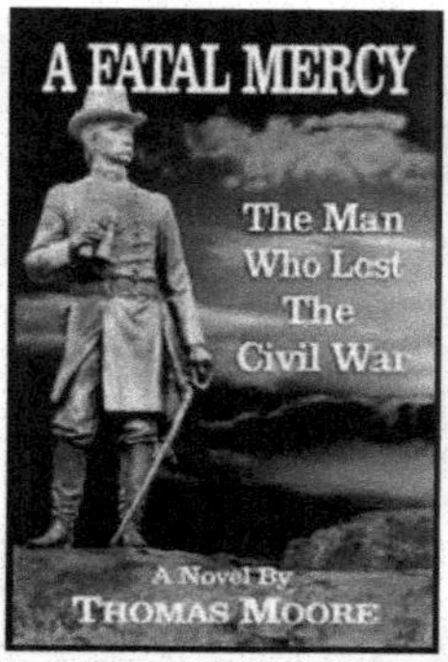

Green Altar (Literary Imprint)

CATHARINE SAVAGE BROSMAN
*An Aesthetic Education
and Other Stories (2nd Ed)*

Chained Tree, Chained Owls: Poems

Aerosols and Other Poems

Partial Memoirs

RANDALL IVEY
*A New England Romance:
And Other Southern Stories*

The Gift of Gab

SUZANNE JOHNSON
Maxcy Gregg's Sporting Journals 1842-1858

JAMES E. KIBLER, JR.
Tiller : Claybank County Series, Vol. 4

The Gentler Gamester

*Beyond The Stone: Poems of Tribute
& Remembrance*

THOMAS MOORE
*A Fatal Mercy:
The Man Who Lost The Civil War*

PERRIN LOVETT
The Substitute, Tom Ironsides 1

KAREN STOKES
Belles

Carolina Twilight

Honor in the Dust

The Immortals

The Soldier's Ghost: A Tale of Charleston

WILLIAM THOMAS
*Runaway Haley:
An Imagined Family Saga*

*The Field of Justice: Moonshine
and Murder in North Georgia*

CLYDE N. WILSON
*Southern Poets and Poems, 1606-1860:
The Land They Loved, Volume 1*

*Confederate Poets and Poems, Vol 1
The Land They Loved, Volume II*

Gold-Bug
(Mystery & Suspense Imprint)

BRANDI PERRY
Splintered: A New Orleans Tale

MARTIN WILSON
To Jekyll and Hide

www.ingramcontent.com/pod-product-compliance
Lightning Source LLC
Chambersburg PA
CBHW050552160426
43199CB00015B/2626